2020

STARS OF SPORTS

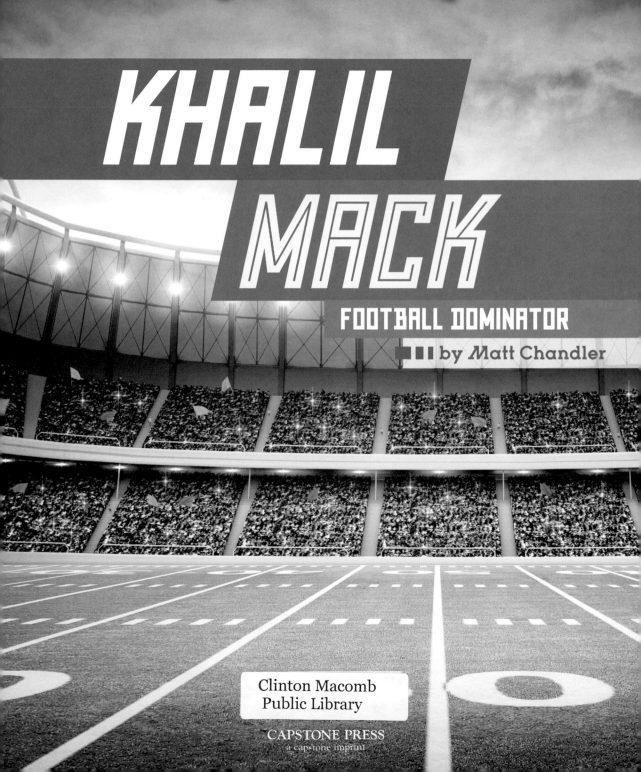

KHALIL MACK

FOOTBALL DOMINATOR

■▮▮ by Matt Chandler

CAPSTONE PRESS
a capstone imprint

Stars of Sports is published by
Capstone Press, a Capstone Imprint
1710 Roe Crest Drive, North Mankato, Minnesota 56003
www.capstonepub.com

**Library of Congress Cataloging-in-Publication Data is available on the Library
of Congress website.**
ISBN: 978-1-5435-9167-5 (library binding)
ISBN: 978-1-5435-9181-1 (ebook PDF)

Summary: As a kid Khalil Mack loved basketball, not football. He didn't even start
playing football until his senior year of high school. That season he racked up 140
tackles, an amazing total. From then on, football became Mack's focus, and he
proved to be a force on the gridiron. In the National Football League, he was named
defensive player of the year in 2016, and today he is widely recognized as one of the
most dominant players in the pro game. It's easy to see why in this engaging, hard-
hitting biography.

Editorial Credits
Christianne Jones, editor; Ashlee Suker, designer; Eric Gohl, media researcher;
Laura Manthe, production specialist

Image Credits
Associated Press: Craig Ruttle, 6, Jeffrey Phelps, 24, Peter Read Miller, 5, Todd
Rosenberg, 25; Getty Images: Kirk Irwin, 13; Newscom: Cal Sport Media/Mike Wulf,
27, Icon SMI/Daniel Gluskoter, 16, 28, Icon SMI/Rich Kane, 14, Icon Sportswire/
Robin Alam, cover, 23, USA Today Sports/Joe Camporeale, 26, USA Today Sports/
Kirby Lee, 21, USA Today Sports/Mike Dinovo, 22, USA Today Sports/Ron Chenoy,
19, ZUMA Press/Mark Konezny, 10, ZUMA Press/Paul Kitagaki Jr, 17, ZUMA Press/
Sarah Grile, 9; Shutterstock: EFKS, 1

Printed in the United States of America.
PA99

TABLE OF CONTENTS

Glossary terms are **BOLD** on first use.

MACK ATTACK

Rookie linebacker Khalil Mack rushed across the line. It was the tenth game of the Oakland Raiders 2014 season. They were playing the San Diego Chargers. So far, the team hadn't won a game.

Mack was a lineman on defense. His job was to break through the offense and get to the quarterback. But so far, he didn't have a single **sack** in the National Football League (NFL). That was about to change.

Chargers tackle King Dunlap blocked Mack and drovc him back. Mack used a spin move to get around him. He wrapped up quarterback Philip Rivers and took him to the ground. That sack was the beginning of Mack's career as one of the most feared pass rushers in the national football league.

Mack in action during his time with the Raiders. 〉〉〉

CHAPTER ONE
QUIET BEGINNINGS

Mack grew up in Fort Pierce, Florida, with his parents and two brothers. Mack was the middle child. He started playing sports with his brothers when he was very young.

Mack was always competitive. He wanted to be the best tackler on the football field. He wanted to be the best shooter on the basketball court. Mack went full speed all the time.

That competitive spirit and hard work helped him become a professional football player.

⟨⟨⟨ Mack brought his mother to the 2014 NFL Draft.

LATE BLOOMER

Mack's first love was basketball. He dreamed of earning a college **scholarship** to play basketball. The scholarship would help pay for school. But he hurt his knee during his sophomore season at Westwood High School. His basketball career was over.

But his scholarship dream was still alive. Mack was already 6 feet 3 inches tall and 220 pounds. Westwood's football coach was impressed with his size. He asked Mack to join the football team. Mack decided to do it. That decision would change his life forever.

Mack averaged 14 tackles per game and had nine sacks in his one season of football. Mack wasn't getting many offers to play college football. Only one college offered Mack a scholarship to play football.

Dunks, Not Defense

Most NFL players start playing football in elementary school. Mack didn't start playing football until his senior year in high school. His main focus was on basketball, hoping to earn a college scholarship.

But one college was enough. Mack left the sunshine of Florida for snowy city of Buffalo in the state of New York. He went to the State University of New York, playing for the Bulls.

〉〉〉 Mack signed to play college football at Buffalo.

CHAPTER TWO
BEASTS OF BUFFALO

Mack arrived in Buffalo in 2009 with a lot to prove. He would have to wait. Mack **redshirted** his first season. He practiced with the team but didn't play in any games.

>>> Mack tackles Eastern Michigan running back Dwayne Priest.

It wasn't until 2010 that he got a chance to play in a game. And in the third game of his **rookie** season, Mack got his first college **sack**. The Bulls were playing the University of Central Florida (UCF).

Mack raced across the line toward UCF quarterback Jeffrey Godfrey. Mack's helmet was ripped from his head. That didn't stop him. He didn't miss a step. He chased down Godfrey from behind for the sack.

The Bulls only won two games that year. But Mack had shown plenty of promise on defense.

FACT

The video game makers at EA Sports ranked Mack's football skills 46 out of 100. Mack chose to wear number 46 in college to remind himself people didn't think he was good enough.

KING OF COLLEGE

For four seasons, Mack led the Bulls' defense and was a feared pass rusher. He racked up 327 tackles and 28.5 sacks.

Mack was best at stopping **opponents** in the **backfield**. His speed meant he was usually in the backfield before the running back had time to make a move.

After his junior year, Mack was seen as a possible fourth round NFL **Draft** pick. His mom told him to return to college and graduate. He could enter the draft the next year. Mack took that advice. And he had a monster senior season.

FACT

The janitor at UB found Mack cleaning the team's locker room late one night. Mack credited his secret cleaning habit to his father, who always taught him to work hard.

<<< Mack and his teammates faced mighty Ohio State in Columbus, Ohio, in 2013.

He made 100 tackles and had 10.5 sacks. His play was noticed by scouts looking for players. Mack would be one of the top picks when new players were chosen in the 2014 NFL Draft.

Mack's senior season changed his future. He was seen as one of the best players in the 2014 draft. A draft expert predicted Mack would be the third pick in the draft that year.

No one knew for sure what would happen. On May 8, 2014, Mack sat in the crowd at Radio City Music Hall in New York City. He waited with his family for his name to be called. Then NFL Commissioner Roger Goodell stepped to the microphone.

"With the fifth pick in the 2014 NFL Draft, the Oakland Raiders select Khalil Mack, linebacker, Buffalo."

⟨⟨⟨ Mack was the fifth pick in the first round of the 2014 NFL Draft.

THE RAIDERS

Mack signed a four-year **contract** with the Oakland Raiders. The deal was worth $18.6 million. The Raiders were not a good football team. They had missed the playoffs for 11 straight seasons. Even the arrival of a defensive giant like Mack couldn't change that.

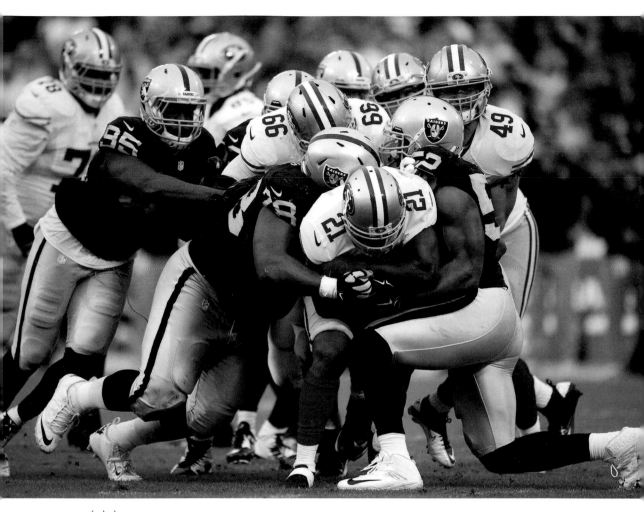

〉〉〉 Mack and teammate Justin Ellis take down San Francisco 49ers running back Frank Gore.

Mack's rookie season in Oakland brought mixed results. The team finished the season with a record of 3-13. Still, Mack proved to be a strong player. He started all 16 games. He had four sacks as a rookie.

Two more seasons would pass before Mack led the Raiders to the playoffs. Fans in Oakland knew they had a special player on defense.

ONE-MAN SHOW

Mack's second season in Oakland ended with another losing record. The Raiders were 7-9. But the big **pass rusher** earned his first Pro Bowl trip, a game only the top players are invtited to. Mack collected 15 sacks. He also forced two **fumbles**.

Mack's best game as a Raider came in December, 2015. The Raiders were in Denver, Colorado, to play the Broncos. Mack sacked Broncos' quarterback Brock Osweiler five times in the game. One sack included a forced fumble in the end zone for a **safety**.

Even with Mack's strong play, the Raiders struggled. They posted losing seasons in three of Mack's four seasons. In his four seasons in Oakland, the team's record was 28-36.

Dynamic Draft Pick

Four players were drafted ahead of Mack in 2014. None of those players appeared in the Pro Bowl during the five years after the draft. Mack earned four Pro Bowl selections in that time.

Mack's five sacks against the Broncos tied Hall of Famer Howie Long for the Raiders' team record.

>>> Mack strips the ball from Denver Broncos quarterback Brock Osweiler in the end zone.

Mack had another Pro Bowl season in 2017. He racked up 10.5 sacks and 78 tackles that season. Mack had played in every game since joining the Raiders. He had also been voted to the Pro Bowl three times. Now he wanted a new **contract**.

Mack sat out the team's off-season workouts. He did not train with the team either. He thought it would force the Raiders to give him a new deal.

The Raiders didn't have the cash to sign Mack to a big deal. They traded him to the Chicago Bears. The Bears gave up two first round draft picks and two other picks in the exchange. They now had the most feared pass rusher in the game.

Mack attempts to block a pass by Chargers ⟩⟩⟩
quarterback Philip Rivers.

MONEY TIME

The Bears signed Mack to a six-year contract. The new deal was worth $141 million. It made Mack the highest paid defensive player in NFL history.

Some people wondered how Mack would do in Chicago. Could he live up to the standard of a team that once had Hall of Fame **linebackers** like Dick Butkus, Mike Singletary, and Brian Urlacher? Would the pressure of the huge contract be too much?

〉〉〉 Mack runs onto the field before a NFC Wild Card playoff game on January 6, 2019.

>>> Mack celebrates with fans after a home win at Soldier Field in Chicago.

A reporter asked Mack if he felt the pressure.

"Absolutely," he said. "I've always thought of myself as the best defensive player in the league. I want to be the best at what I do."

Mack had only one week to prepare for his first game as a Bear. The heat was on.

MONSTER GAME

The Bears kicked off the 2018 season on the road against the Green Bay Packers, playing at Lambeau Field. Mack took over the game with three minutes left in the first half.

Packers' quarterback DeShone Kizer was driving his team down the field. Mack raced through the offensive line on a third down play. As he pulled Kizer to the ground for a sack, Mack stripped the ball loose. He ended the Packers' scoring drive.

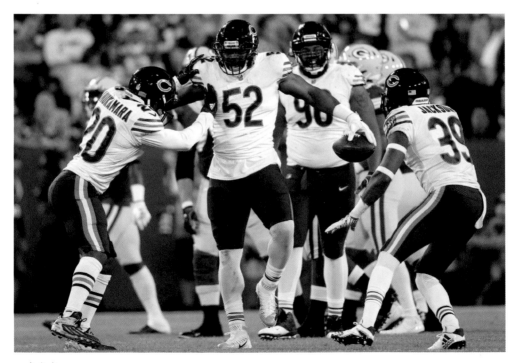

>>> Mack celebrates after recovering a fumble.

>>> Mack charges toward the end zone against the Packers.

Mack stunned the crowd at Lambeau Field less than three minutes later. Green Bay had one last scoring chance before the half. Kizer tossed a pass over the middle. Mack stepped in front of the receiver and grabbed the ball. He raced 28 yards for a touchdown. It was the perfect start with his new team.

RETURN TO THE PLAYOFFS

Mack was having another Pro Bowl season in 2018. Then he injured his ankle in the sixth game of the season. He missed two games. They were the first he missed in his NFL career.

Mack returned and recorded 7.5 more sacks and 27 tackles in the final eight games of the season. The Bears went 7-1 and returned to the playoffs.

〉〉〉 Cardinals quarterback Sam Bradford fumbles the ball after a solid hit from Mack.

>>> Mack takes down Eagles quarterback Nick Foles during an NFL Playoff Game.

The Bears lost in the first round of the playoffs. But Mack had given the fans in Chicago a lot to cheer about. He also earned his fourth Pro Bowl trip.

MACK TO THE FUTURE

Does Mack have what it takes to be the greatest of all time? Maybe.

Bruce Smith holds the NFL record with 200 career sacks. Through his first five seasons, Smith had 57.5 sacks. Mack had 53 sacks in his first five seasons. Smith played 19 years in the NFL. Today, players like Mack rarely play for so long because the game is so physical.

Mack is an elite player. His averages of three forced fumbles and more than ten sacks per season prove that. Whether he is among the best linebackers of all time will be argued once his playing days are over. Football fans hope that won't be anytime soon.

TIMELINE

1991 born in Fort Pierce, Florida, on February 22

2006 suffers a serious knee injury playing high school basketball

2008 joins the football team at Westwood High School

2009 graduates high school and accepts a scholarship to the State University of New York at Buffalo to play football

2011 leads the UB Bulls team in sacks

2013 wins 2013 MAC Defensive Player of the Year

2013 named second team All-American football player by the Associated Press

2014 picked by the Oakland Raiders in the NFL Draft; he was chosen fifth overall

2014 records first NFL sack on November 16 against the San Diego Chargers

2015 ties a Raiders' team record with five sacks in a single game on December 13

2016 intercepts Cam Newton and returns the pass for his first NFL touchdown

2017 starts the first playoff game of his career and makes eight tackles

2018 traded to the Chicago Bears on September 1

GLOSSARY

BACKFIELD (BAK-feeld)—the area of play behind the offensive or defensive line

CONTRACT (KAHN-trakt)—a legal agreement

FUMBLE (FUHM-buhl)—when a player drops the ball or it is knocked out of his or her hands by another player

LINEBACKER (LINE-bak-ur)—a defensive player normally positioned behind the line of scrimmage, but in front of the safeties

OPPONENT (uh-POH-nuhnt)—a person who competes against another person

PASS RUSHER (PASS RUH-shr)—a defensive player who charges toward the quarterback at the line of scrimmage in an attempt to prevent a pass

REDSHIRTED (RED-shur-tuhd)—practiced with a team but didn't participate in games; allows college athletes to develop skills for another year without losing eligibility

ROOKIE (RUK-ee)—a first-year player

SACK (SAK)—when a defensive player tackles the opposing quarterback behind the line of scrimmage

SAFETY (SAYF-tee)—when a player is tackled behind his own goal line; the defensive team is awarded two points and the ball

SCHOLARSHIP (SKOL-ur-ship)—money given to a student to pay for school

READ MORE

Lyon, Drew. *A Superfan's Guide to Pro Football Teams.* North Mankato, MN: Capstone Press, 2018.

Omoth, Tyler. *Dak Prescott: Football Superstar.* North Mankato, MN: Capstone Press, 2019.

Rieken, Kristie. *Mega Watt: J.J. Watt's Surge to Greatness.* Chicago: Triumph Books, 2015.

INTERNET SITES

National Football League
http://www.nfl.com

Pro Football Hall of Fame
http://www.profootballhof.com

Sports Illustrated Kids: Football
https://www.sikids.com/football

INDEX